C0-CCE-010

ASKLIPIOS-EPIDAUROS AND THEIR MUSEUM

DIMITRIOS PAPASTAMOU

*DF
19
.A65
vol. 13*

ST. JOSEPH'S UNIVERSITY

3 9353 00306 3896

APOLLO EDITIONS

The following guides have been published by the APOLLON Publishers and can be obtained at the corresponding archaeological sites:

By the Archaeologists

Athens Byzantine Museum — Manolis Chatzidakis

Minoan Civilisation and Knossos Palace — Sonia di Neuhoff

The Acropolis and its Museum — M. Brouscaris

The Acropolis — M. Brouscaris

Copper Items of the Athens National Archaeological Museum — Basil G. Callipolitis, Efie Touloupa

Delphi — Sonia di Neuhoff

Ancient Olympia — Dora Karageorga

Ancient Corinth — Sonia di Neuhoff

Marble Masterpieces of the Athens Archaeological Museum — Dimitrios Papastamou

Vases of the Athens National Archaeological Museum — Barbara Philippaki

Cycladic Collection of the Athens National Archaeological Museum — Efie Sapouna-Sakkelaraki

Epidaurus

To be published

Mycenaean Collection of the Athens National Archaeological Museum — John Sakkelarakis

Lindos — Sonia di Neuhoff

Mycenae-Mycenaean Art

Corfou

Cover: *Front:* The Theatre.
         Back: Asklipios (plaster-cast).
Text: Dimitrios Papastamou.
Photographs: «Hannibal».
Published by E. Tzaferis, S.A. - 52, rue Fokionos Négri - Athens.
Printed by H. Fournier, S.A. - Vitoria - Spain.

INTRODUCTION

Whether it is a distant tour or a single visit, travel of any sort to archaeological sites in Greece, requires the traveller to prepare himself mentally and spiritually for a confrontation with the past and a revival in his mind's eye of scenes and events, linking him with whatever place he is going to visit. He is then ready to hear again the rhapsodies of ancient times, to experience the noise and clamour of preparation for the Games in the clearing between the Alpheios and Kladeos rivers, or the spectators' applause for the victors of the Olympic contests. In Delphi he is overwhelmed by the landscape, in Epidauros and Kos he is struck by the achievements of medical science and by the variety of healing processes.

This book is his help and guide in communicating with the past and in deriving the upmost pleasure from his unique experience. It opens the way to restoration of ruined monuments, of the religious, social and artistic creations of antiquity, and imparts to them the authentic stamp of history.

The first travellers were Crusaders, passing through Greece on their way to the Holy Land. In the comprehensive and informative records they made the German Rudolf von Sudheim and the Italian Nicolo da Martoni have left us many observations of what we might call «touristic interest».

Accounts by 15th century writers of their travels in Greece are often very detailed. The Florentine Buondelmonti journeyed to the Islands of the Archipelago in fulfilment of a plan he had previously made, and collected manuscripts, which may be read to this day in the Laurenziana Library in Florence.

The first traveller, however, to show a really scientific interest in Greece was Kyriakos (F. Gregorovius) who arrived in Athens from Ancona. He was followed by the artist Squarcione from Padua who, if tradition is to be believed, was the person who gave Mantegna his first opportunity to study and copy such ancient monuments, as Squarcione had managed to make plaster casts of and remove from Athens.

The 16th century is the century of the French traveller. Pierre Bolon visited Greece to study its flora and fauna as well as its ancient ruins, while Seigneur de Borderié recorded his admiration and impressions of the country in a poem, that would have appealed to the women of his day.

The greatest number of travellers to Greece in the early part of the 17th century came from Italy and many of them were artists. There were also other men of intellect, whose sketches and records of their travels in Greece, undertaken either privately or as envoys of foreign powers, deserve to be mentioned. Peiresc, Louis Des Hayes and Du Loire did everything they could to make Greece more widely known. From the correspondence that passed between two distinguished painters of the first half of the 17th century, Rubens and Poussin, we know that a scientific interest in the country was slowly awakening. One of the outstanding travellers of the time was a scientist and intellectual, the Frenchman Doctor Jacob Spon. He toured Central Greece, Attica, Corinth and the Argolid in the company of two Englishmen, Wheler and Vermon. Compared with Peiresc's publications, Spon's account of his travels is considered to be a monumental work of description and scientific observation. We owe to Peiresc and Spon and other unknown French travellers a variety of information of touristic and archaeological interest, such as an account of the destruction of the Parthenon and records of the whereabouts of wonderful examples of ancient art that had all but been lost to sight. Nevertheless, during the last years of the 17th century (the period of Baroque) and the first half of the 18th (Rococo) there is no instance at all of study or travel in Greece or of any cultural contact with the country. It was not until about 1750 that European culture began to react against the Rococo style. In 1764 Winckelmann, with his passion and love for the ancient Greek world,

4

published his «Geschichte der Kunst des Altertums», while two years earlier the Englishmen Stewart and Kevett had produced «The Antiquities of Athens».

These two publications were the spark that set alight the old love and admiration and interest in all Greek things. Though Winckelmann's early death prevented him from realising his dream of visiting Greece, many of his fellow countrymen followed his lead. The most important of them was Von Riedesel who collected valuable archaeological and travel information.

The intellectual climate engendered by Winckelmann in Germany stirred up an interest in and affection for ancient Greek art, which once again challenged the fashion for Rococo, a style that prevailed throughout the 18th century.

Then 18th century closes with the publication by the Sicilian author, Scrofani, of a book that was translated into French, English and German. In it he gives the most penetrating account one imagines any Italian traveller could write under the inspiration of affection and admiration for the people who 2,300 years before had adorned his native island of Sicily with the finest examples of ancient Greek architecture.

In the same way that the first resurgence of the spirit of ancient Greece, the Italian Renaissance, came about mainly through observation of ancient Roman art and through cultural contact with it, so did the second revival in the form of 17th century French classicism. But from the second half of the 18th century the way was clear for western Europeans to enjoy cultural contact with Greece itself. The most important exponents of this concept of contact are chiefly German humanists and philosophers.

Late 19th century authors of impressions and studies of Greece wrote under the influence of the theories of Bachofen, Rohde and Nietzsche. The effect can be seen in every account attempted of an ancient site or sanctuary. Johann Jacob Bachofen ends his description of the Sanctuary of Asklipios with the following words: «When one reflects on these things, this narrow, peaceful valley reveals itself to be the equal of the greatest centres of Hellenic religious festivals, like Delphi and Olympia».

Despite all the ugly intrusions of our civilization that have swamped the sacred site of the Asklipios, we ourselves can experience Bachofen's admiration today if by a painstaking process of selection and a spiritual approach to the sanctity of the place we reconstruct in our mind's eye all that transpired there.

«A miracle is the most beloved child of faith».
GOETHE

ASKLIPIOS

The ancient Greeks attributed to their all-powerful gods not only the intangible and insoluble mysteries of human existence, but also every manifestation of nature that affected their environment and transient life.

Thus it was, in their view, that earth-shaking Poseidon caused the dry land to quake and the seas to be rough, and smiling Aphrodite bestowed or withheld love and cupid's kiss; that the busy artificer Hephaistos forged his wonderful weapons and ingenious tools and the marksman Ares destroyed young men in battle.

Asklipios, the curer of illnesses, was not numbered among the twelve Olympian gods, nor was he considered one of the more ancient deities like cloud, gathering Zeus whose cult was spread by the earliest Greek conquerors (see E. SIMON, *Die Götter der Griecken*, 1964, p. 14 ff.) or like blue-eyed Athena, of Minoan-Mycenean origin (see A. FURUMARK, *Opuscula Artheniensia*, 6, 1958, p. 98), or silver bowed Apollo who was introduced from Asia Minor and fast became «the most Greek of all the Gods» (M. P. NILSSON, *The Minoan-Mycenaean Religion*, p. 485 ff.).

It is difficult to accept that Asklipios was worshipped as a divinity in prehistoric times. If one is guided by archaeological research and discoveries, one is inclined rather to the view that the worship of Asklipios spread as the worship of a hero of only local cult importance. Homer, the earliest of literary sources, makes no mention of Asklipios as a god in either the Iliad or the Odyssey or in the Hymns. The poet uses his name as the patronymic of the heroes Machaon and Podaleirios, supposedly his sons, who participated in the sack of Troy as leaders of the forces from Trikki and other small cities of Thessaly (*Iliad*, IV, 194, XI 518, 11731).

The somewhat later epic poet Hesiod knew more than Homer did about the divine origin of Asklipios. From him we learn that his mother was the daughter of Phlegys, Koronis, who deceived the god Apollo though she was expecting a child by him. Informed by a crow of Koronis's faithlessness, Apollo cursed the bird for bringing him such unwelcome news and changed its white plumage to black. His sister Artemis brought about the death of Koronis. Apollo rescued his son Asklipios from her dead doby which had been commited to the flames of a pyre, and carried him to Mount Pelion where he delivered him to Cheiron, a Centaur and tutor. From him Asklipios learned the use of herbs and various healing prescriptions.

The employment of the god Asklipios's miraculous medicine and of his gift of healing, which extended even to the restoring of the dead to life and thus to the upsetting of the balance maintained between the living and the dead, was the cause of Zeus striking him dead with a thunderbolt. Pindar, another Beotian poet but much later than Hesiod, repeats and in a way authenticates, what Hesiod related in his lost work, the «Ioeai».

The sources mentioned and the earliest finds associated with the cult of Asklipios rather suggest he was originally a local hero in the region of Thessaly who enjoyed the power of healing. Excavations at Trikkala have uncovered two sites which may have been the sites of an Asklipios or shrine of Asklipios. Perhaps the worship of Asklipios as a hero had its origin at Trikkala in archaic times and slowly spread southwards. The worship of Asklipios made its first appearance in Athens in the 5th century B.C., the earliest historical evidence we have of it, at about the time Athens and Piraeus were struck by a cholera epidemic to which Pericles fell victim. The fame of Asklipios's healing powers had already spread among the inhabitants when his worship began first in Piraeus and shortly after in Athens. The tragic poet Sophocles, then a priest of the cult of Alkon, better-known as Amynos, a hero and gifted healer, accepted the appearance of the god Asklipion in Athens. A temple was later erected in his honour at the foot of the Acropolis. In earlier times he had occupied a fitting place in the sanctuary of his father Apollo at Delphi. A sacred area had been set aside there for his worship in the 5th century B.C. Later, in the second half of the 4th century, special buildings were erected to provide for the comfort of great crowds of faithful pilgrims.

Sikyon also accepted the introduction of the cult of Asklipios, as did Corinth where a famous Asklipion was built. Excavations in Corinth have led to the discovery of large quantities of terracotta replicas of parts of the human body, the grateful ex-votos or the supplicatory offerings of the desperately ill, whose faith had brought them to this sanctuary in search of a cure.

The best known Asklipion where therapeutic treatment was scientifically given was in Kos. Hippocrates was the most celebrated of the famous teachers in the island's medical schools.

Another renowned Asklipion was founded at Pergamon. The one in Rome was a precise copy of the Athenian shrine and its building was similarly owed to a fearful epidemic. When a raging and uncontrollable epidemic struck the city in 293 B.C. the Sibyls prophesied in the Sibylline books that «the epidemic will end only when Asklipios, god of medicine, is brought from Epidauros to Rome».

An official delegation was sent to Epidauros and, as Ovid

relates in his Metamorphoses (Book XV, p. 622 ff.) the god was duly taken back to Rome in the guise of a snake. The religious and cult dedication of the temple of Asklipios and Hygeia on the island surrounded by the waters of the River Tiber took place on the 1st of January, 291 B.C.

The worship of Asklipios can be traced right down to the fifth century after Christ (R. DELBRUECK, *Die Consular-diptychen*, 1929, 215 ff.).

Despite the proscription in 392 A.C. by the Emperor Theodosius I of idolatrous practices, it seems this particular cult was not completely stamped out. Magic, the evil eye and superstition were the direct spiritual links employed in the fanatical and sacred communion with the god.

Every locality sacred to Asklipios, every Asklipion had its own special manner of administring treatment that owed its origin to the divinity. In this respect Epidauros and Kos are the very opposite of one another.

In the course of excavations made by the Greek archaeologists Cavvadias and Papadimitriou, four of the six inscribed columns erected within the sacred area of Epidauros were discovered. These columns tell us about the healing methods employed in more, than seven hundred cases (see R. HERZOG, *Die Wunderheilungen von Epidaurus*, *Philologus Suppl.* XXII, 3, 1931).

They also make it clear that there was no organized medical, staff at Epidauros, as there was in Kos; treatment was prescribed by the priests and their assistants, and the patient paid appropriate fees. The god, usually appearing as a snake, worked his cure, through dreams.

Two examples of a cure are provided by the cases of Agamide, a barren woman of Kea, who came and slept in the sanctuary, dreamt that a snake settled on her stomach and later gave birth to five children; and of a mute girl who was running in the wood when suddenly she saw a snake approaching, sliding down the trunk of a tree. Terrified, she shouted out for her mother and father, and left the place cured of her dumbness.

The explanation of these occurrences and man's faith in them is evidenced by the large number of relief ex-votos or offerings —most of them on display in the National Museum in Athens— that represent instances of Asklipios' divine intervention (see U. HAUSMANN, *Kunst und Heiltum, Untersuchungen zu den gr. Asklepios-reliefs*, 1948).

The earliest appearance of Asklipios in representational forms of art occurs towards the end of the 5th century B.C. More representative still are the sculptured figures portraying the god as a venerable, kindly and gentle being. Commoner scenes show Asklipios on votive reliefs in the act of appearing to the afflicted, of working a cure or receiving offerings (sacrifices). (See G. EDELSTEIN, *Asklepios*, 1964). An exception to the usual representation of the god Asklipios, familiar to us only through Roman copies, is to be seen in his statue, now in the National Archaeological Museum of Athens, found in Piraeus and known as the statue of Asklipios of Mounichia-Este (see D. PAPASTAMOS, *Marble Masterpieces in the National Archaeological Museum*, 1971, No. 58). This statue resembles in technique the head of Asklipios from Melos in the collection of the British Museum (see G. LIPPOLD, *HBAW* III, 1, 1950, 259, fig. 95, 2).

Statues of the god were carved by Alcamenes in Mantinea and Kanachos in Sikyon. Literary sources indicate that Kiphisidotos, Skopas and Vryaxis all worked on sculptures depicting the god. A gold and ivory seated figure of Asklipios was made by Thrasymides for the temple at Epidauros, the sculptor being clearly influenced by the idol of Zeus in Olympia.

Most artists represented the god as a venerable old man with thick and wavy hair and heavily bearded (only the sculptor Kanachos portrayed a beardless Asklipios, see I. FINK, *Hermes* 80, 1952, 111 ff.).

11

The god wears his himation or cloak in the same style as it was worn by learned teachers in the 5th and 4th centuries leaving most of the breast uncovered (fig. 4). The god leans on a knotted staff propped under his left armpit and with a snake entwined around it.

It is mainly in relief carvings that we observe a hemispherical mound close to the figure of Asklipios. This is the omphalos or, navel (see *Revue Belge de Numismatique*, 97, 1951, 5 ff.). The mythological significance of the omphalos, held to be the centre of the earth and closely connected with Delphi, has been completely lost sight of, and its meaning has been widely accepted as the symbol of a burial (see M. ANDRONIKOS, *Archaeological Bulletin* 17, 1961-1962, 176 ff.). The theory that the representation of an omphalos by the side of Asklipios is connected with a primitive form of his cult as a hero with curative powers in the guise of a snake on top of a tomb is therefore more likely to be accurate (see H. V. HERMANN, *Omphalos*, 1959, 65 ff.).

Other representations portray Asklipios accompanied by Telesphoros, personification of omnipotent power and god of mysterious and magical healing (see *Pausanias*, 2, II, 7; also W. DEONNA, *Coll. Latomus*, 21, 1955).

More often, however, the god Asklipios is shown together with the female goddess, Hygeia, symbolising his brilliant gifts as a healer.

Hygeia, whom most later writers refer to as the daughter of Asklipios (*Pausanias*, 1, 23, 4, 34, 3; *Pliny* 35, 11, 40), is a comparative latecomer to Greek pantheon. For this reason Hygeia is not mentioned anywhere in Greek mythology. From the 6th century B.C. we find the goddess Athena frequently referred to in inscriptions as Athena-Hygeia. It can be said with some certainty that the worship of Hygeia began in the 4th century B.C. at Epidauros and thence spread to other regions.

Of the secondary figures mentioned above in association

12

with Asklipios in various art forms, the only symbolic one is the snake, which both as a figure and as a symbol has inherited its religious and mythological character from Creto-Mycenean worship.

Along with its appearance after the Dorian invasion as in some manner connected with the dead (see K. KÜBLER, *Kerameikos*, V 1, p. 27, note 66 and related bibliography), it is met with as a demon or evil spirit (for example, as Python at Delphi, Kychreus at Salamina, Kekrops and Erechtheus at Athens), as well as possessing the attribute of a companion of gods (of Athena, Demeter, Dionysos, Zeus Meilichios and Sosipolis) [see E. KÜSTER, *Die Schlange in der gr. Kunst und Religion*, 1913]. The snake is something more than a symbol and companion of Asklipios: it is his original form. From this follows the correct modern view that in the beginning he was worshipped as a snake, as a kind of spirit with both healling and death-dealing attributes. The god emerged later until eventually he was being worshipped in human form, the snake remaining his constant companion and symbol. These facts set the stage for an analysis of the relationship between Asklipios and the snake, but this is not the place for such an analysis.

As a symbol, the snake is represented and concerned with psychopathic, erotic and healing situations. These are related in turn with the god Asklipios's appearances in the course of dreams (see R. HERZOG, *Die Wunderheilungen von Epidaurus, Philologus Suppl.*, XXII 3, 1931).

Cures of barrenness cannot in any way be related with C. G. Jung and S. Freud's erotic psychoanalytic symbol, referred to as the «libido».

The tortoise, a long-lived animal known in antiquity, is also connected with Asklipios (see H. KELLER, *Tierwelt* II, 247-259), despite its close ties with Hermes (see M. WEGNER, *Das Musikleben der Griechen*, 1949, 14 ff.).

The festive hymn of Asklipios, as of Apollo, was the Paean,

13

a fact that points on the one hand to his descent from Apollo and, on the other to the deeper significance of the Paean itself, which may be said to have been a form of supplication.

The same conclusion can be drawn from the Odyssey (19, 455), namely, that through the efficacy of the hymn chanted the blood ceased to flow from the wound: «By the use of magic they stopped the black blood from flowing».

And so the faithful worshipped Asklipios and their worship endured for more than a 1,000 years. Moreover, the disciples of Asklipios inheriting from their fathers the title and craft of healers, still preserve today skills and prescriptions, surgical instruments and operations dating back to an age to which belong the sacred ruins you are on the point of visiting.

THE MUSEUM

A bust standing a few yards distant from the entrance to the small local Museum is a reminder for the visitor of the archaeologist, Panayotis, Cavvadias, who dedicated himself to discovering ancient Epidauros.

The first small room contains inscriptions in which are recorded medical prescriptions, treatments and miraculous cures, as well as financial records of the cost of buildings and constructions. Medical and surgical instruments are displayed in the upper part of a show-case of the room, oil lamps and small terracotta offerings in the lower (fig. 1, 3).

Scrapers and ear-picks, scalpels, probes and forceps are only a few of the medical tools found on the sacred site and exhibited here. They belong to the Hellenistic period.

Opposite the show-case of instruments, whose scientific use and origin are confirmed by earlier finds in Kos and Epidauros, is an inscription by the poet Isyllos of Epidauros, author of five poems dedicated to Asklipios. He flourished around 280 B.C. (see E. DIEHL, *Anthologia Lyrica*, II).

A statue stands in each corner of the small room. Three of them represent as many different classes of Roman society, while the fourth is of a woman, dating probably to the last years of the Hellenistic age or else to the opening of the Roman period.

The heads of the male figures were carved separately from the bodies and then fixed to them; they are representational. One shows a Roman wearing a toga, the formal, as it were, national attire of the time; another portrays a Roman general, and the third an ordinary Roman citizen.

Marble roof gutters (simai) and rain-spouts (hydrorroai) in the shape of roaring lion-heads, through the open mouths of which water poured off the roofs of buildings, are displayed on projections from all four walls.

The painted terracotta gutters and eave tiles (hegemones)

15

with floral decorations, displayed below them, are from the roof of the inner sanctuary.

Cult offerings and pedimental statuary (in this instance casts) are displayed in the second room, along with architectural members of sanctuary buildings.

Above the doorway in the east wall is a section of the roof guttering of the 4th B.C. Temple of Asklipios, again with waterspouts in the form of lion-heads.

On the left as you enter is a badly damaged head of the emperor Hadrian. It is a copy of the type of head of the emperor found in the Therme Museum in Rome (see M. WEGNER, *Hadrian*, 1956, Rollockenfrisur). To the right is a fine representational head of a bearded man of late imperial Roman times. Among the headless statues in the front part of the room are two figures of the goddess Athena wearing across her breast an aegis (shield) portraying a gorgon's head, one of the goddess Hygeia with a snake, and one of a Roman general in his toga. Shortage of space makes it impractical to show some really noteworthy finds made during the last 20 years in both the sanctuary and the surrounding area. We are therefore restricted here to the display and description of plaster casts of original works now in the National Archaeological Museum of Athens (see DIM. PAPASTAMOS, *Marble Masterpieces of the National Archaeological Museum*, 1971). One of these casts is of the god Asklipios (fig. 4) and shows him in the stand already described (see p. 11). In his expression are reflected both love of mankind and gravity of manner.

The upcast and far-seeing eyes, the rendering of the thick head of hair give him an almost wild and leonine appearance. Though they fall short of the marks of grandeur sought after by the artist, they nevertheless measure up to the popular image of time of the compassionate god of the 4th century B.C.

Other marble casts are the four lower groups of which

the originals are exhibited in the National Archaeological Museum of Athens: «Avrai» (Breezes) Nos. 157 and 156; «Niki» (Victory), No. 155; and «Hygeia» (Health), No. 299.

We frequently come across the name of one of the most distinguished artists of the 4th century B.C., the sculptor Timotheos, in descriptions and aesthetic appreciations of the sculpture decorating buildings on the site of Epidauros. Among the works attributed to him are the ones already mentioned. These groups of mounted «Breezes» (fig. 6) used to decorate the corners of a roof pediment; they were in fact the akroteria of the temple of Asklipios. In all probability they represent the soft, life-giving breezes which were so indispensable to the Sanatorium of Asklipios. The wind ruffling the garments and the variation of body surfaces beneath the remarkably worked dress material may not belong to a pioneer technique of art, but they indicate the deceptive ease of the carving and the artistic achievement of the sculptor.

The statue of Niki (fig. 5), seen here holding a partridge, symbol of health (according to N. Yalouris) suggests a similar aetherial quality.

The figure of Hygeia (fig. 7) is closer to Timotheos' technique. Introducing entirely new features, such as the inclination of the body, the offering of food (?) to the snake and the interrelationship of the body and the garment clothing it, the sculptor presents a combination of the two most widely known symbolic personifications of the god Asklipios. The four compositions just mentioned may be dated to about 380 B.C.

Immediately following the marble cast of the goddess Hygeia (to the right on entering) is a display of some architectural features of buildings that stood in the sanctuary of Epidauros. The first come from the portico of the sanctuary, to which the roads from Troezine, Argos and the ancient port of Epidauros all lead. The portico is the northernmost building in the sanctuary (fig. 33, 1). The architectural remains of the Gymnasium portico (fig. 33, 18), displayed on both sides of the door to the Room C, ionic to the left (fig. 8) and corinthian to the right, suggest its former elegance and grandeur.

On the wall above the ionic architectural fragments of the Gymnasium portico is a frieze (triglyphs and metopes) possibly from the temple of Artemis but more probably from an altar. One of the metopes shows Athina with Asklipios.

Immediately on the right after entering Room C down foursteps is a partial reconstruction of the entablature of the temple of Asklipios, built in the doric order (fig. 9). Above the door is a section of the cornice that framed the face of the temple pediment (in this instance part of one of the inclined sides, without the usual dentil decoration). An example of the doric columns of the temple of Asklipios may be seen in the reconstructed column of the entablature next to it. The task of rebuilding the temple of Asklipios began about 380 B.C. The architect Theodotos worked on it, but four different stylistic conventions may be distinguished in the pediment decoration. There are references in inscriptions to the names Timotheos, Theodotos, Ektoridas and, fourthly, to Theo..., a fact that makes the attribution of particular works to any one of them problematical.

The temple of Asklipios covered a ground area of 11.76 × 23.06 m, making it one of the smallest temples built in the doric manner. A colonnade comprising 6 columns at the ends and 11 on the side, enclosed a temple without an opisthodomos and featuring a floor of contrasting colours, an effect already known from the temples of Zeus at Olympia and Apollo at Delos and achieved by the use of alternate dark and white marble.

Various items of information about the building, decoration and embellishment of the monument are given in inscriptions.

A highly decorated door made of wood, ivory and studded with nails of gold, the work of one Thrasymidis, closed off the shrine itself which contained a gold and ivory cult statue of the god Asklipios seated. A lot of relief sculptures show the god in a similar position. In all probability are contemporary copies of the famous cult statue itself (fig. 10, 11).

Statuary found in front of the two short sides of the temple (each with six columns) was readily identified as pediment sculptures and akroteria.

It was at first thought that the eastern pediment represented the battle of the Centaurs and Lapiths. But in the light of more recent finds and studies made by several archaeologists (J. CROME, B. SCHLÖRB, N. YALOURIS) it is nowadays accepted that it represented the battle between the Greeks and Trojans (The Fall of Troy). There is no doubt that the western pediment portrayed the battle of the Amazons. The sculptures surviving from the two pediments are now in the room, known as the Epidauros room, specially reserved for them at the National Archaeological Museum in Athens (fig. 12).

At the corners of the building (fig. 5, 6) stood the statues already mentioned of the Avrai and of Niki, carved in Parian marble.

The metopes (10 in number) situated beneath the eaves and supported by triglyphs (11) were decorated with beautifully sculpted rosettes. The Museum contains a partial reconstruction of a length of these metopes.

The temple of Artemis, another doric structure (fig. 13), stood near to the temple of Asklipios within the sanctuary area. It had only six columns on the front side and two in ante. Inside, ten columns enclosed the cult statue of the goddess, who was worshipped also under the name of Hecate in close association with the cult of Asklipios (see TH. KRANS, *Hekate*, 1960).

Typical of the decoration of this small shrine are the gut-

19

ter-spouts, of which the corner ones were in the shape of a pig's head and those in between of a dog's-head (fig. 13).

The remaining space in Room C is filled with elaborate architectural members of the Tholos, the most graceful building within the sanctuary of Epidauros (fig. 14, 15, 16). They start with the doorjambs, richly decorated with rosettes.

Inscriptions recording the costs of labour and building material once again come to our help in dating the start of construction work on the Tholos to around 360 B.C. and its completion to about 320 B.C. The contractor was a sculptor named Polyklitos whose dexterity, traditional style and technical adaptability in contrasting materials and colours make one seriously wonder if he were a grandson or nephew of the great 5th century Polyklitos (see R. BIANCHI-BANDINELLI, *Policleto, Quad. per lo studio dell'Archaeol.* I, 1938. Also D. SCHULTZ, *Hermes*, 83, 1955, 200-220 and C. WEICKERT, in *Thieme-Becker, Kunstlerlexicon*, 1933).

Forerunners of this Tholos were: a) the Tholos at Delphi, dating to the early 6th century, of which remains were found in the course of the excavation of the Sikyon Treasury; b) the Athens Tholos in the Kerameikos, a building of about 530 B.C., but without a colonnade; c) the Athens Tholos in the Agora (Prytaneion), about 465 B.C. and also without a colonnade; and d) the Delphi Tholos in the sanctuary of Athena Pronaia, built about 380 B.C. by the architect Theodoros the Phocian which had a diameter of 21.68 metres (the inner sanctuary was 14.65 metres in diameter). The cellar or crypt of the Tholos (fig. 20) survives and can be seen when visiting the ruins.

It consists of three concentric circular passages and was used probably as a reptile house for the sacred snake to which frequent references are made in religious inscriptions at Epidauros and whose guise was often assumed by the god Asklipios.

A doric colonnade of 26 columns surrounded the circular shrine, while its interior was adorned with 14 Corinthian columns forming an elaborate enclosure (fig. 14). The roof of the enclosure was covered with marble panels of superb workmanship, the centre of each one of which lying within a border formed by a double band of astragals (huckle-bone or bead pattern) was decorated with beautifully sculpted acanthus buds and leaves with a central rosette motif. The empty space left between the panels on account of the circular structural shape of the building was filled with a spiral pattern of garlands (fig. 17, 21, 22, 23).

The metopes of the colonnade, instead of having a narrative or illustrative motif, were decorated with large rosettes in relief. A spiral design of acanthus stems, flowers and lion heads adorned the marble cornice which encircled the building and served to prevent rainwater from pouring over the face of the triglyphs and metopes.

The interior or sanctuary of the Tholos was illuminated through a large doorway, the jambs of which were richly embellished with a pattern of flowers, rosettes and volutes of astragals in a manner reminiscent of the Erectheion. There is no evidence of any windows.

The Tholos, referred to in one inscription as the Thymele (see F. ROBERT, *Thymele*, 1939), was the most elaborate feature of the whole sanctuary. This impression was conveyed in part by the use of building materials from a variety of sources (marble from Paros and Pentelis, limestone from Elefsis and local quarries) and in part by the contrasting of colours and decorative motifs which contrived to give the building a festive and fanciful appearance.

Pausanias' account tells us that the interior was covered with pictorial scenes which included Pafsios' famous painting of Methi, a young maiden drinking from a glass vessel of such transparent quality, that the traveller Pausanias singled it out for praise.

21

A capital found close to the Tholos in almost its original condition (fig. 18, 19) was the work of Polyklitos the younger. There can be no doubt that this was the model used by the stonemasons who carved the 14 Corinthian capitals that decorated the interior of the Tholos.

Nowhere else have excavations brought to light a more elaborately decorated building than the Tholos at Epidauros (P. CAVVADIAS, *Fouilles d'Epidaure*, 1893). The sculpture work is rich in volutes and scrolls, astragals and acanthus leaves, rosettes and flower stems, all picked out in colours harmonizing with the gilded wooden ceiling, the murals of the sanctuary interior and the richly ornamented door. The building is considered to be not only one of the most beautiful of ancient edifices but also to be the finest of all Tholos structures known up to that time. Why it was rebuilt is a mystery. The amazing wealth of its architectural decoration, its striking appearance and the contrasting plainness of the temple of Asklipios lead to the assumption that the Tholos was used for some special cult object. This object may well have had to do with the engendering, by means of the impressive grandeur of its character, of a spiritual sense of conviction of the plausibility of the legends surrounding the birth of the god Asklipios at Epidauros, his tomb there and the emergence of the sacred snake from it.

THE SANCTUARY OF EPIDAUROS

The footpath leading off to the left of the Museum towards the sanctuary of Asklipios is not one taken by the faithful in antiquity. They used another running in the opposite direction from the north side of the shrine where the Propylaion stood (fig. 33, 1) with its double row of Corinthian and Ionic columns, not Doric and Ionic as in the Propylaia of the Acropolis of Athens.

The first ruins one meets following the footpath from the Museum are the remains of a large hostelry (fig. 33, 19).

The hostelry was a square building with sides 76.30 metres long and two floors containing 160 rooms arranged around four courtyards (fig. 33, 19). Moving westwards we come to the ruins of a bath lying immediately to the south of the Gymnasium (76 × 70 m) which had an inner courtyard adorned with 60 columns. In Roman times an odeon, of which there remain traces of tiers of seats and the stage, was constructed inside this courtyard.

Passing through yet another portico we can see on our right a ward for invalids and the so-called Stoa (or arcade) of Kotys (?) (fig. 33, 19).

The temple of Artemis, of which there is a reconstruction in the Museum, lies a little further north. Just beyond it is the earliest ward of all (fig. 33, 10). We are now within the Sanctuary of Asklipios itself, to which mostly pilgrims and suppliants for the favours and an apparition of the god resorted. We can see the altar set up to the god and beside it the shrine (fig. 33, 22), that contained his statue to which pilgrims brought their valuable gifts and dedicated their terracota or metal offerings representing the afflicted parts of their bodies for which they sought a cure.

North of the temple and parallel to its longer side formed by 11 columns stood the dormitory or avaton, as it was referred to inscriptions (fig. 33, 10). This had 29 ionic columns

23

in front of it, whereas 13 interior columns supported the roof. It was divided into two long aisles in which the sick spent the night awaiting the apparition of the god in a dream.

On the east side of the avaton is a well 17 metres deep, a carefully built wall retaining its upper part. Water from the well was drunk for its efficacy as a purge and remedy. The well was surrounded with columns and tablets on which the god's miraculous interventions and cures were recorded.

In front of this well, on the level of the avaton, stood the Tholos described in an earlier section on the Museum (see p. 21). The three concentric and labyrinthine corridors survive to this day in an excellent state of preservation (fig. 33, 12).

Continuing northwards and passing in front of the Temple of Asklipios, there is a complex of buildings to the left which are Roman baths and beyond them are the Sacred Way and the Propylon (fig. 33, 7). Straight ahead, some 30 metres distant, are the ruins of an early Christian church dedicated to Saint John (fig. 33, 2).

Returning towards the Museum and abreast of the Palaistra or arena (fig. 33, 18) on the side facing the public road lies the Stadium (fig. 33, 11). This was connected with the Sanctuary by an underground passageway. We can get a fairly clear idea of what the 181 metres long Stadium looked like, but the remains of the seating of the so-called theatre running down the length of the arena lead us to presume that most spectators, as at Olympia, had to sit on the ground. Both its length and the position of the stone starting and finishing lines provide evidence for the dating of the Stadium to the Hellenistic period (a Roman Stadium was 177.55 metres long).

The ruins of a chariot race track have been found about three kilometres southwest of the Stadium.

Between 1948 and 1951 the Sanctuary of Apollo Maleata was excavated on Mount Kynortion lying to the northwest

24

of the Sanctuary of Asklipios (see J. PAPADIMITRIOU, *Records of the Archaeological Society*, 1950-1951).

It was on this sacred site in the late 6th century B.C. that the healing and succouring god was first worshipped. But clear evidence of his worship, resting on historical and chronological proof, is available from only the 5th century on.

Most of the architectural ruins, enough to allow a general reconstruction of the sanctuary of Asklipios (fig. 33), belong to temples and philanthropic buildings, comprising the only charitable foundation in 4th and 3rd century B.C. of ancient Greece.

The first building on the site was the relatively small temple of the deity, followed closely by the unusually magnificent circular structure of the Tholos; after which came in succession the theatre, throughout antiquity reputed to be the most beautiful anywhere; the splendidly impressive Propylaia, terminating the sacred road from the habour of Epidauros; the Gymnasium, Stadium and hostelry and other buildings designed for the treatment of the sick.

THE THEATRE

«Τὰ πρῶτα τῶν ἄλλων ἠνεγκάμεθα, ὦ Σώκρατες» —«I came first, Socrates», was Ion's reply when asked how he got on in the Epidauros musical contest, held in honour of Asklipios, which he had entered (Plato's «Ion»).

While it is Pindar (518-446 B.C.) who has most to tell us about the athletic games held at Epidauros, it is the dialogue in Platon's «Ion» that is our chief source of information about the musical contests that occurred there. Reading this dialogue we learn about the customs and appearance of the rhapsodists, who took part in them. The rhapsodists (of whom Ion was one), to whom Kleisthenes, ruler of Sikyon in the first half of the 6th century B.C., forbade entrance to his city, flourished in the 5th century B.C. They used to travel from city and during their public appearances, when they recited from memory, would wear a golden crown on their head and costumes heavy with jewelry (see W. SCHADEWALDT, *Von Homer Welt und Werk*, 1951, 54 ff. Also KL. STÄHLER, *Eine Unbekannte Pelike des Eucharides Malers*, 1967, 6 ff.).

If the information given us in the introduction to the dialogue between Socrates and Ion is not an indication of the starting point of the dialogue and of the direction to be taken by the ideas Plato projects in the course of their discussion but is evidence of the particular celebrations in which Ion participated as a rhapsodist, then there must have been an orchestra, predating the Epidauros theatre we know, from the floor of which Ion would have recited before the judges and audience and carried off the first prize.

However, no reference is made to any such archaeological finds nor are they even surmised in analytical studies of the building of the theatre at Epidauros (see A. v. GERKAN, W. MÜLLER-WIENER, *Das Theater von Epidaurus*, 1961, 76-84. For general studies of the theatre see C. ANTI, *Teatri*

Greci Arcaici, 1947 and the *Lexikon der Antike, Kunst II*, 328-336 in which there is a complete bibliography by K. G. KAHLER).

The present-day appearance of the theatre is the result of recent restoration, carried out in the years 1958-1959 under the supervision of the General Direction of Antiquities of Greece (fig. 24, 27, 28, 29, 30, 33 and 34).

According to Pausanias we owe to Polyklitos the theatre's acoustical perfection, recognised also in ancient times, its architectural balance and aesthetic integration what the foothills of Mount Kynortion, qualities still enjoyed by the visitor today and particularly by the spectator of the dramas performed in the course of the annual Epidauros festival. «Polyklitos was the creator of this theatre and the surrounding building», Polyklitos who was the nephew or grandson, as already mentioned, of the great sculptor of the classical age (see R. BIANCHI-BANDINELLI, *Policleto*, 1938. Also E. BERGER, *Enciclopedia Universale dell'Arte* 10, 1963, 773-781 and E. BOER, *Lexicon der Antike*, 2, 198 ff. which also contains a bibliography).

Nevertheless, the view lately put forward by A. v. GERKAN that the theatre was built during the first quarter of the 3rd century B.C., perhaps under the direction of an architect called Polyklitos, who must obviously have had not connection with Polyklitos the sculptor, seems more likely to be true.

During the first phase of the theatre's construction the tiers of seats had a capacity of 6,200 spectators. Later, in the first half of the 2nd century B.C. the upper tiers containing 20 rows were added. This increased the number of spectators to about 14,300 and gave the theatre its final and present-day appearance which was unaffected by restoration work done by the Romans who erected the statue of the Empress Livia in the proscenium wing.

The tiers contain three front rows of seats for officials

and fifty-two rows for the public. They are divided in the lower part into 13 and in the upper into 23 blocks. The uppermost row of seats is 59 metres from the orchestra and 22.56 metres above the level of the front row. The orchestra has a diameter of 9.77 metres.

There used to be a narrow room, built in the ionic order, in front of the stage in which were kept various panels of painted scenery. The portals, at the beginning of the side-approaches, of which the doorposts remain, also belonged to the ionic order.

As noted above, it is not known if the musical contests in which the rhapsodist Ion received first prize were held in this particular theatre. But there is no doubt at all that performances of plays by the tragic dramatists Aeschylus, Sophocles and Euripedes, whose works were favoured in the 4th century B.C. not only by the public but also by actors, are part of the history of the theatre of Epidauros.

Apart from tragedies and comedies, mime-plays and pantomime, both branches of dramatic art, were presented at Epidauros. Though these two kinds of performances were products of the Greek theatre they were introduced to the stage only in the time of Augustus. The abandonment of the theatre has been dated to the 3rd century B.C., followed a little while later by the abandonment, destruction and gradual overgrowth of the Sanctuary of Asklipios.

It was in 1881 that the Greek archaeologist, P. Cavvadias began the systematic excavations that lasted to 1887 and brought to light the remarkable sanctuary of Asklipios at Epidauros. His excavations gave rise to new theories, based on scientific observation and research, regarding on the one hand the religio-social influence of the cult of the god Asklipios (see W. F. OTTO, *Theophania*, 1956), and on the other the technical and architectural contributions made by the 4th century B.C.

EPILOGUE

When one walks down Kynortion hill one cannot but admire the oldest finds associated with the cult of a hero held in honour in the region of Epidauros. As darkness envelops the Sanctuary and theatre a divine peace falls on the place, a prelude to the apparition of the god.

To look on those ruins today is to feel oneself living in the age when Epidauros was at the height of its fame and to envisage the place in its pristine state. Circular and rectangular structures, columns and platforms take shape before the eyes. Ruined temples are restored to their ancient form, the avaton fills once more with transfixed and frightened beings lying in readiness for the apparition of the god. The one-eyed and the blind are there to be cured by the god rubbing ointment he has made into their empty eye-sockets; and the lame, too, who on the morrow will throw away their crutches; and a bald man from Lesbos whose head will once again be covered with hair, thanks to the god's miraculous intervention.

The more seriously afflicted are also here, like the old man with a stomach ulcer and the young Spartan girl suffering from dropsy. They and others like them await their cure by surgery.

Purged by the waters of the sacred spring (fig. 33, 11) they sleep in expectation of a remedy: the arthritic, the dumb, the lepers, the itchy and barren women. A lame and bow-legged man lies in front of the sanctuary waiting for the help of the god who will cure him without fail by mounting his chariot and driving his horses over him until his limbs regain their natural shape. These and many other pious invalids seek the alleviation of their sufferings by the god.

There are, too, some invalids who harbour evil thoughts, like the blind man who will not pay a fee for his remedy even if it works. Him the god will blind again and will restore his sight to him only when he has promised that he will not repeat his action in future.

The temple servant moves about among the patients snuffing out the lamps. Sacred night-time has fallen at last. The god Asklipios will appear to each in a dream and give them all a sign of the manner of their cure. (In Aristophanes' *Pluto*, act. 3, scene 2, the chorus, Karion and Chremylos' wife describe such a sacred night). Some of the inscriptions that have been found offer an assortment of medical advice. The god advises the sick to drink hemlock and lime and to bathe in cold water. To those suffering from pleurisy he recommends compresses of hemlock soaked in wine; he advises those coughing blood to eat for three days the kernels of pine-cones prepared with honey.

Rich gifts were made to the god and large medical fees were paid. Many pilgrims wrote verses and poems, hymns and praises to the glory of the god Asklipios. One suppliant named Isyllos, on the instructions of Apollo, father of Asklipios, extolled the miracles and compiled the genealogy of the doctor-god (see p. 15) whose cult persisted for a thousand years and gave rise through folk medicine to the most distinguished of all lines of scientists, whose successors today still wear his emblem.

The most popular Asklipion was undoubtedly the one at Epidauros. The most famous, however, at which treatment followed scientific diagnosis, was in Kos. It was there, among the practitioners of Asklipian skills, that the renowned Hippocrates (27 Agrianion 460 B.C.), son of Heraklides, another of the god's disciples, was to be found the embodiment of a true science (see M. POHLENZ, *Gestalten aus Hellas*, 1950, VIII, 329-351).

LIST OF FIGURES

Fig. 1 - Inscription concerning the cure of the sick.
Fig. 2 - Medical and surgical instruments.
Fig. 3 - Terracotta votive vases and small idols.
Fig. 4 - Asklipios (plaster-cast).
Fig. 5 - Nike, a roof-statue (akroterion) from the temple of As-
         klipios (National Archaeological Museum, Athens).
Fig. 6 - Avra, roof-statue (akroterion) from the temple of Askli-
         pios (National Archaeological Museum, Athens).
Fig. 7 - Hygeia (National Archaeological Museum, Athens).
Fig. 8 - Reconstruction of the Gymnasium Propylaia (ionic order).
Fig. 9 - Section of the entablature of the Temple of Asklipios.
Fig. 10 - Asklipios seated on a throne (National Archaeological
         Museum, Athens).
Fig. 11 - Asklipios (National Archaeological Museum, Athens).
Fig. 12 - A mounted Amazon from the pediment of the temple of
         Asklipios (National Archaeological Museum, Athens).
Fig. 13 - Section of the entablature of the temple of Artemis.
Fig. 14 - Reconstruction of part of the colonnade of the Tholos.
Fig. 15 - Corinthian capital from the columns of the Tholos.
Fig. 16 - Details of the decoration of the Tholos.
Fig. 17 - Section of the roof soffits of the Tholos.
Fig. 18 - The Corinthian capital used as a model.
Fig. 19 - Detail of previous figure.
Fig. 20 - View of the ruins of the Tholos.
Fig. 21 - Section of the roof of the Tholos showing soffits.
Fig. 22 - Detail of fig. 17.
Fig. 23 - Detail of fig. 21.
Fig. 24 - Ruins of the sanctuary of Asklipios.
Fig. 25 - The Sanctuary of Asklipios.
Fig. 26 - The Stadium.
Fig. 27 - The Theatre.
Fig. 28 - The Theatre.
Fig. 29 - The Theatre.
Fig. 30 - The Theatre.
Fig. 31 - Ex-voto offering by patients seeking a cure for maladies
         of the ear.
Fig. 32 - Reconstruction of the sanctuary of Epidauros by P. CAV-
         VADIAS.

31

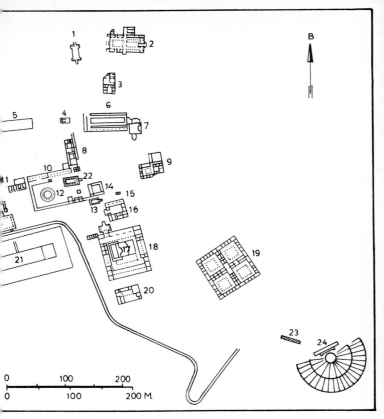

1. Propylaia.
2. Church.
3. Roman House.
4. Temple of Aphrodite.
5. Cistern.
6. Stoa (colonnade).
7. Roman Baths.
8. Baths and Library.
9. Sanctuary of the egyptian gods.
10. Inner Sanctuary.
11. Spring.
12. Tholos.
13. Temple of Artemis.
14. Priests' House.
15. Temple of Themis.
16. Stoa of Kotys.
17. Odeion.
18. Gymnasium.
19. Guest-House.
20. Greek Baths.
21. Stadium.
22. Temple of Asklipios.
23. Museum.
24. Theatre.

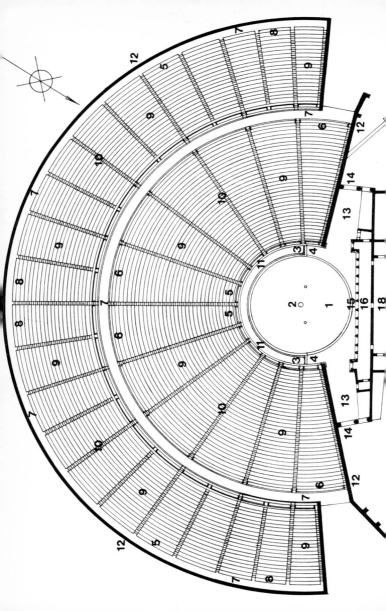

PLAN OF THEATRE

1) Orchestra. A circular and level space in the middle of the theatre within which the rhapsodists and chorus performed.
2) Thymele. The centre of the orchestra; the rhapsodists stood on the steps leading up to it.
3) Evripos. A rainwater conduit.
4) Kathodos. Descending passageway.
5) Koilon. Auditorium, part natural part constructed.
6) Lower auditorium.
7) Diazomata. Uninterrupted gangways separating the upper and lower parts of the auditorium.
8) Epitheatron. The upper tiers of seats.
9) Kerkides. Semicircular continuous rows of seating.
10) Klimakes. Stone steps giving access to spectators' seating.
11) Proedria. The front row of the lower tiers, reserved for «men worthy of their country» only.
12) Buttress walls supporting the auditorium structure.
13) Parodoi. Entrances for the use of the public and the chorus.
14) Pylones. Open spaces immediately in front of the entrances.
15) Proskinion. Proscenium: the front of the stage (see No. 18), on which the rhapsodist or actor stood.
16) Logeion. Space in front of the proscenium where the actors or chorus stood.
17) Paraskinia. The wings or spaces to the left and right of the stage where actors prepared for their entry and where later various stage properties were kept (see Megalopolis Theatre).
18) Skene. The stage or that part of the theatre where the actors stood and played.

ΜΙΟΥΛΙΟΣΑΠΕΛΛΑΣΙΔΡΙΕΥΣΜΥΛΑΣΕΥΣΜΕΤΕΤΙΕΜΦΘΗΝ
ΥΠΟΤΟΥΘΕΟΥΠΟΛΛΑΚΙΣΕΙΣΝΟΣΟΥΣΕΝΠΙΠΤΩΝΚΑΙΑΠΕΨΙ
ΑΙΣΧΡΩΜΕΝΟΣΚΑΤΑΔΗΠΟΝΤΔΛΟΥΝΕΝΑΙΠΕΙΝΗΕΚΕΛΕΥΣΕΝ
ΔΙΕΜΠΟΛΛΑΔΓΕΙΠΕΣΘΑΙΕΤΙΠΑΡΕΓΕΝΟΜΗΝΕΠΙΘΙΕΡΩΣ
ΞΕΛΕΥΣΙΝΕΙΚΑΔΥΘΜΕΡΑΣΣΥΝΚΑΛΥΨΑΣΘΑΙΤΗΝΚΕΦΑΛΗΝ
ΝΑΙΣΟΜΒΡΩΠΕΓΕΝΟΝΤΟΥΡΟΝΚΑΙΑΡΤΟΝΠΡΟΛΑΒΕΙΝΣΕΛΕΙ
ΝΑΜΕΤΑΦΡΙΛΑΚΟΣΑΥΤΟΝΔΙΑΥΙΟΥΛΑΟΥΘΑΙΔΙΟΜΟΓΥΜΝΑΣΕ
ΘΑΙΚΙΠΙΟΥΤΠΡΟΛΑΜΒΑΝΕΙΝΤΑΔΚΡΕΙΣΥΔΟΡΑΠΟΒΡΕΞΠΙΠΡΟΣ
ΑΙΣΑΚΟΛΙΣΕΝΥΑΝΕΙΟΠΕΩΤΡΙΒΕΣΘΑΙΠΟΠΟΙΧΟΙΠΕΡΙΠΑΤΟΥΧΡΗ
ΘΛΙΥΠΕΡΟΔΑΣΠΡΑΙΣΑΦΗΤΗΛΩΣΑΣΘΛΙΑΝΥΠΟΛΗΠΟΝΠΕΡΙ
ΠΑΤΕΙΝΠΡΙΝΕΜΒΗΝΑΙΕΝΠΟΙΘΒΑΛΛΑΝΕΙΟΣΕΙΣΤΟΘΕΡΜΟΝΥΔΩΡ
ΘΙΝΟΝΤΕΡΙΧΕΑΣΘΑΙΜΟΝΟΝΛΟΥΣΑΣΘΑΙΚΑΙΑΤΤΙΚΗΝΔΥΝΑΙ
ΘΙΒΑΛΛΑΝΕΙΚΟΙΝΗΘΥΣΔΙΑΣΚΑΗΤΙΛΟΗΠΤΙΟΝΗΕΛΕΥΣΕΙΝΙΑΙΣ
ΑΛΛΑΜΕΤΑΓΓΕΑΠΟΣΠΡΟΛΑΒΕΙΝΜΙΑΔΕΗΜΕΡΑΤΠΙΟΝΤΟΣΜΟΥΤΑ
ΑΜΟΝΟΝΕΙΠΕΝΜΕΔΙΕΜΒΑΛΛΕΙΣΤΟΓΑΛΛΑΙΝΑΔΥΝΗΤΑΙΔΙΑΚΟΙ
ΤΕΙΝΕΠΕΙΔΕΕΛΕΗΘΗΝΥΠΟΤΟΥΘΕΟΥΘΑΠΤΟΝΜΕΛΑΠΟΛΥΣΑΙΩΜΗΝΑ
ΥΙΚΝΙΑΛΣΙΝΚΕΧΡΕΙΜΕΝΟΣΟΛΟΣΕΞΙΕΝΑΙΚΑΤΑΤΑΣΑΚΟΑΣΕΚΤΥ
ΒΑΤΟΥΠΑΙΔΑΡΙΟΝΑΓΗΤΕΙΣΘΛΙΘΥΜΙΑΤΗΡΙΟΝΕΧΟΝΑΤΜΙΤΟΙΣ
ΑΠΟΝΙΕΡΙΑΛΛΕΓΕΙΝΤΕΘΕΡΑΠΕΥΣΑΙΧΡΗΔΕΑΠΟΛΙΔΟΝΑΙΤΑΤΙΛΤΙΔ
ΔΙΕΠΟΙΗΣΑΣΙΔΟΝΚΑΙΧΡΕΙΜΕΝΟΣΜΕΝΠΟΣΑΛΣΙΚΑΠΟΙΝΑΠΥ
ΤΙΕΡΟΙΗΛΤΛΣΑΛΟΥΜΕΝΟΣΔΕΟΥΚΗΔΤΗΣΔΤΑΥΤΑΕΝΕΝΝΕΑΗΜ
ΑΙΣΑΦΟΥΔΑΣΟΝΗΨΑΤΟΔΕΜΟΥΚΑΙΤΗΣΔΕΞΙΑΣΧΙΡΟΣΚΑΙΤΟΥ
ΙΑΣΤΟΥΤΗΔΔΕΓΕΤΗΣΗΜΕΡΑΣΤΠΙΟΝΤΟΣΜΟΥΦΛΟΞΑΝΑΔΡΑΜΩΝ
ΛΕΠΙΣΦΛΕΥΣΕΤΗΝΧΕΙΡΑΛΩΣΚΑΙΦΛΥΚΤΑΙΝΑΣΕΞΑΝΘΗΣΑΙΜΕΤΟ
ΠΙΟΝΔΕΥΤΗΣΗΧΕΙΡΕΓΕΝΕΤΟΕΠΙΜΕΙΝΑΝΤΙΜΟΙΑΝΗΘΟΝΜΕ
ΕΛΑΙΟΥΧΡΗΣΑΣΘΑΙΠΟΣΤΗΝΚΕΦΑΛΛΑΓΙΑΝΕΙΠΕΝΟΥΜΗΝΗΛ
ΣΥΝΤΗΝΚΕΦΑΛΗΣΥΓΕΒΗΟΥΝΦΙΛΟΛΟΓΗΣΑΝΤΙΜΟΙΣΙΝΠΑΗ
ΟΘΗΝΑΙΧΡΗΣΑΜΕΝΟΣΤΟΕΛΑΙΟΑΠΗΛΑΓΗΝΤΗΣΚΕΦΑΛΛΑΤΙ
ΣΑΝΑΓΑΡΓΑΡΙΣΘΛΙΨΥΧΡΟΠΡΟΣΤΗΝΣΤΑΦΥΛΗΝΚΑΙΓΑΡΠΕΡΙ
ΟΤΟΥΠΑΡΕΚΑΛΕΣΑΤΟΝΘΕΟΝΠΟΛΥΤΟΚΑΠΠΡΟΣΠΑΡΙΣΘΜΙΑΣΕΚ
ΕΥΣΕΡΗΔΕΚΑΙΑΝΑΓΡΑΨΑΠΣΑΥΤΑΧΑΡΙΝΕΙΛΩΣΚΑΙΥΤΙΗΣΓΕ
ΝΟΜΕΝΙΟΣΑΠΗΛΛΑΓΗΝ

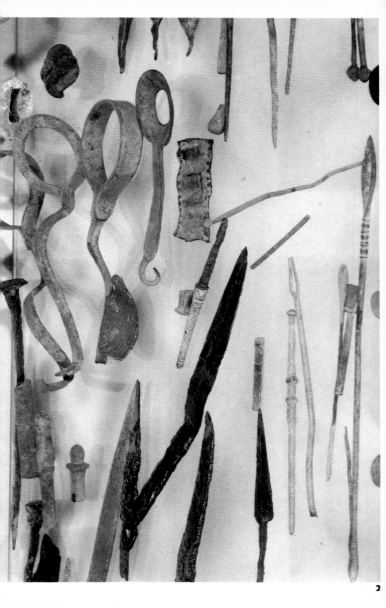

4

9

14

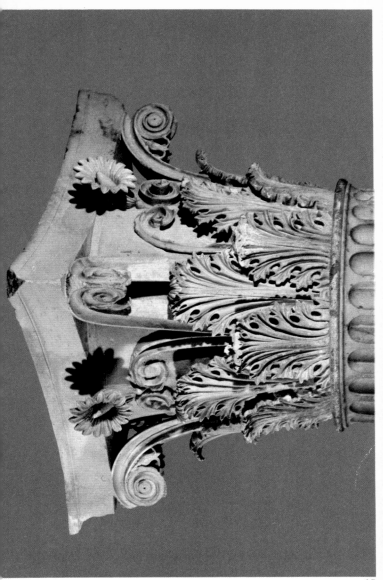

15